MW01094816

# From the Closet to the Pulpit

WAYNE MCGHIE

All Scripture quotations, unless otherwise indicated, are taken from the Holy Bible, New International Version®, NIV®. Copyright ©1973, 1978, 1984, 2011 by Biblica, Inc.™ Used by permission of Zondervan. All rights reserved worldwide. www.zondervan.com The "NIV" and "New International Version" are trademarks registered in the United States Patent and Trademark Office by Biblica, Inc.™

Scripture taken from the New King James Version®. Copyright © 1982 by Thomas Nelson. Used by permission. All rights reserved.

ISBN-13: 978-1724514417
ISBN-10: 1724514415

# DEDICATION

To the people who seek a godly answer to one of the most vocal issues of our time, amidst the noise of the public arena, I believe you'll find among these pages the answers that you're looking for.

# Contents

## ACKNOWLEDGMENTS

Many thanks to my dear wife, Hope Messengers, my editor, and all the people who have partnered with me in making this book possible. Most of all, thanks to my Savior Jesus Christ who has a Plan for each of us.

# INTRODUCTION

A friend once asked, would God send a person to hell for loving someone of the same sex? She was a Christian who happened to also be bisexual. We spent the next several months between lunch together, private chats and email messages, discussing this very personal subject. Some of the issues we explored are covered in this book.

Everyone needs to love and be loved. My goal is to present factual data with sensitivity and respect, while maintaining the integrity of the information. If that is your experience as you read this book, I have succeeded. We may not agree in every area, that's ok. My friend and I didn't agree on everything. Hopefully, those are the areas where my extensive research will be of greatest benefit.

We will navigate through issues that concern millions of people throughout the world, including same-sex marriage, transgender questions, homophobia, sexual orientation, and biblical principles that relate to these issues. Some of the information will surprise you.

For example, being gay or transgender does not make a person less of an accountant, doctor, lawyer, soldier, or a neighbor. So why is the suicide rate so high for gay and transgender people? Considering everyone's need to be loved, why draw a line at same-sex relationships? People are destroyed for lack of knowledge (Hosea 4:6, NKJV), but information cures ignorance.

We will cover much in the chapters ahead. Let's begin our conversation!

~ Wayne McGhie

# 1   THE SIN OF SODOM AND GOMORRAH

Her name was Shame, but not today. Like a timid doe she emerged, from darkness into the city lights. The stained Spanx hugged the curves of her contoured body; she was naked with her clothes on. The street lights shone upon the face of the watchers, whose ignorant stares gave worship. But she was hungry, and the night hid a tear that streamed onto her reddened lips.

"What's your price?" a stranger asked.

"Peace, love and hope," she replied.

"How about five hundred bucks?"

"I could use that too," she sighed.

She held the stranger close, as they returned to her quiet sanctuary.

"Your life is sin!" a preacher cried.

"Life is no sin!" was her reply. "Your god has made me who I am, and you have damned me just for being."

The preacher's voice was silenced by the cheers of the crowd; some of them belonged to his church. In love and compassion, they felt driven to protect her from those who would harm her. "Love is never wrong," they said, "because God loves everyone."

"So, what's your name?" her partner asked.

She lifted her eyes and smiled. "Today, my name is Gay."

She closed her door and fed her hungry soul with the attentions of her lover, as the sounds filled the night, and echoed into the heavens until God heard, and considered it all: "Love is never wrong... God loves everyone."

-~<+>~-

Would you disagree that God loves people who happen to be lesbian, gay, bisexual or transgender? How would you respond to my Christian friend's question, "Will God send me to hell for loving someone of the same sex?" Or do you feel these issues are too complicated? As with many truths, the answer begins with a story, but there will be twists along the way!

Sodom and Gomorrah were two renowned cities of the Bible, recorded in Genesis 18 and 19. While on His way to visit these cities, God told Abraham, "The outcry against Sodom and Gomorrah is so great and their sin so grievous" (Gen. 18:20). Then He left to verify the existence of the sin He spoke of.

Upon confirming this great sin in the cities, God sent angels to destroy Sodom and Gomorrah in one of the most stunning acts of destruction recorded in the Bible. But what *really* was the grievous sin that brought God from His throne, down to earth? Consider the events that unfolded during the angel's visit, in Genesis 19.

> The two angels arrived at Sodom in the evening, and Lot was sitting in the gateway of the city. When he saw them, he got up to meet them and

bowed down with his face to the ground. 'My lords,' he said, 'please turn aside to your servant's house. You can wash your feet and spend the night and then go on your way early in the morning' …. Before they had gone to bed, all the men from every part of the city of Sodom—both young and old—surrounded the house.

They called to Lot, 'Where are the men who came to you tonight? Bring them out to us so that we can have sex with them.' Lot went outside to meet them and shut the door behind him and said, 'No, my friends. Don't do this wicked thing.

'Look, I have two daughters who have never slept with a man. Let me bring them out to you, and you can do what you like with them. But don't do anything to these men, for they have come under the protection of my roof' … They kept bringing pressure on Lot and moved forward to break down the door.

But [the angels] inside reached out and pulled Lot back into the house and … struck the men who were at the door of the house, young and old, with blindness so that they could not find the door.

The two men said to Lot, 'Do you have anyone else here … Get them out of here, because we are going to destroy this place. The outcry to the Lord against its people is so great that he has sent us to destroy it.'

Verses 24 to 25 record the sobering conclusion.

Then the Lord rained sulfur and fire out of the sky from the Lord on Sodom and Gomorrah, overthrowing those cities, all of the plain, and everyone who lived in the cities. He also destroyed the plants that grew out of the ground.

We'll refer to these incidents throughout the book, and unpack these events. So, what was the grievous sin? The arguments surround the following: lack of hospitality, rape, or homosexuality. But there is a fourth possibility.

### Lack of Hospitality

Recall the angels' words in verse 13, "The outcry to the Lord against its people is so great that *he has sent us to destroy it.*" Sodom and Gomorrah were destroyed because of *what God saw* when He visited, not what the angels experienced. The focus on the angels is the fatal flaw in the "lack of hospitality" conclusion. The angels were merely soldiers on assignment to fulfill a decision that was already made.

This means if the men of Sodom and Gomorrah had rolled out the red carpet and offered the angels beer and a barbecue, they would still have destroyed the cities. They could not do otherwise without being guilty of disobeying God's direct order. Sodom and Gomorrah were not destroyed for lack of hospitality. That being the case, could the grievous sin have been rape?

## Rape

The argument for rape is based on the incident where every man from every part of the city surrounded Lot's home, demanding that he bring the angels out so they could "have sex with them" (Gen. 19:4). Lot refused their demand (Gen. 19:9), but they insisted.

> 'Get out of our way,' they replied. 'This fellow came here as a foreigner, and now he wants to play the judge! We'll treat you worse than them.' They kept bringing pressure on Lot and moved forward to break down the door.

Recall that Lot had also offered his daughters to the men but they refused. Rape has to be consummated in order to have occurred. Dictionary.com defines rape as, "Unlawful sexual intercourse or any other sexual penetration of the vagina, anus, or mouth of another person, with or without force, by a sex organ, other body part, or foreign object, without the consent of the victim."

The men were not guilty of rape because no rape

happened in any of these incidents, though they clearly intended to rape the angels. But intent is not rape. So, with rape and lack of hospitality out of the question, can we now conclude that the crowd of men was homosexual?

No.

### Homosexuality

Angels are always referred to as masculine in the Bible, but most of us have also seen them depicted as female in literature. Arguably, they are more often depicted as female than male. Could the men of Sodom and Gomorrah have been lusting after female angels, making it a heterosexual crowd? Let the men answer that question.

In chapter 19 verse 5 the crowd called out to Lot, "Where are *the men* who came to you tonight? Bring them out to us so that we can have sex with them." In the mind of those men, the angels were male, and now we have clarity.

Sodom and Gomorrah were destroyed by God, including its children and the very plants that grew on the ground, to erase a forbidden influence. That influence was homosexuality. In all the records of human history, there has never been an act more anti-gay on such a scale as this.

Was this homophobia?

# 2 HOMOPHOBIA

That word, *homophobia*. The very sound bears the stench of intolerance and hatred; social diseases. Homophobia has been defined, but the meaning remains elusive because it attaches itself to any concept that opposes the LGBT worldview. Consequently, to be anti-gay is to be homophobic, even for moral or religious reasons. But what is homophobia?

Vocabulary.com defines it as, "A hatred of or prejudice against gay, lesbian, bisexual, or transgender people." It explains, "The word homophobia literally means 'fear of homosexual people,' from the Greek roots homos, 'one and the same,' and phobia, 'irrational fear of,' and its original use was closer to 'fear by heterosexuals of being thought to be gay.'"

Every scripture in the Bible that mentions homosexuality, does so in the negative, pronouncing death and destruction on consenting individuals for loving members of their own sex. What would be the outcry if a leader in any city of the world today destroyed its citizens for practicing homosexuality: from San Francisco to Amsterdam; from Atlanta to Paris? One judgment would be loudest: homophobia! Does Almighty God have a "fear of homosexual people"?

If God is Almighty then He cannot fear, else He would neither be God nor Almighty. Therefore, it is impossible for fear to be His motivation. How about, "a hatred or prejudice against gay, lesbian, bisexual, or transgender people"? John 3:16 says God loves the world so much that He sent Jesus, His Son, to die for all humanity, so we could live with Him forever. Who would sacrifice his child for someone he hates? Yet, gaze upon the charred bodies in Sodom and Gomorrah. Do you see love?

This we know: Jesus willingly died for mankind. He said, "No one takes [my life] from me, but I lay it down of my own accord. I have authority to lay it down and authority to take it up again. This command I received from my Father" (John 10:18).

As your mind surveys the smoldering streets, do you tell yourself, if I were God, I would never do such a thing? If you do, doesn't that make you holier than God, otherwise, by whose standard do you judge Him? Or could it be that you've missed something?

A phobia is "an intense and irrational fear of something. If seeing a particular object makes you scream and jump on top of a table, then you likely suffer from a phobia" (Vocabulary.com). Here is how they explain it:

> The thing to remember about phobia is that it describes an *irrational* fear. If you're afraid of a black widow spider, for example, that's not a phobia — it's just smart, because the spider is poisonous. If you're afraid of all spiders, however, and the sight of a harmless daddy long legs spider has you shaking in terror, then you may have a phobia. In this case, it's a phobia *because your reaction is irrational* (emphasis added).

Considering that a phobia is irrational fear, how might an arachnophobe behave around spiders? Could you identify an agoraphobic person who was in a crowded place? How would you identify a homophobic person who was in the presence of a gay person?

Many individuals, some gays included, genuinely hate the LGBT lifestyle. And there are people who oppose it but would go out of their way to help their gay neighbor. Compelled by love, Jesus suffered on the cross to save all humanity from sin because God—a judge—*must* judge sin.

The destruction of Sodom and Gomorrah was God's judgment against sin, not hatred of people. Therefore, it could never represent the fear and hatred that is homophobia. To deem it so would be to sanctify a vice because what God does is the standard for all that is holy. Jesus died for people, because of sin; to save the one, and to destroy the other.

Similarly, Christians are commanded to oppose sin, in all its forms, by teaching the Gospel and by living a godly life. Christ has never taught His disciples to be hateful, even toward those who hate them. Therefore, it is impossible for a person to be hateful to anyone, yet remain a faithful Christian.

It is dangerous to categorically label all anti-gay positions "homophobic," including when communicated from a pulpit, and here is why. By applying this label indiscriminately, individuals who disagree on moral or religious grounds are identified equally with those who would do harm. As a result, it is difficult to distinguish between those who legitimately disagree, and those who hate; an environment that conceals homophobia.

## Violence Against Gays

Jesse Marczyk, Ph.D., and other colleagues conducted research regarding violence against gays, in light of the June 2016 shooting at the Pulse nightclub in Orlando, Florida. Their question was, does repressed homosexual appetites result in homophobia?

Some speculated that the shooter harbored homosexual desires he was trying to repress, that these urges involved visiting gay nightclubs and using gay dating apps to communicate, and that the shooting resulted from frustration over these unmet drives, directed against others. But the Orlando Sentinel found something different.[1]

> Federal investigators have scoured Omar Mateen's laptop computer, cell phone and the trail of communications he left behind and so far have found no evidence that he led a secret gay life, according to officials who spoke on the condition of anonymity about the ongoing investigation. They've also reviewed the electronic devices of men who said they'd communicated with him on gay dating apps and so far have found no link... they've found no photographs, text messages, smart phone apps

---

[1] Rene Stutzman & Paul Brinkmann. Federal officials: No evidence gunman used gay apps, looked at gay porn, had boyfriends.
http://www.orlandosentinel.com/news/pulse-orlando-nightclub-shooting/os-orlando-nightclub-shooting-gay-evidence-lacking-20160623-story.html

---

or gay pornography that suggest Mateen was gay or was trying to find a gay lover.

The evidence by the Federal investigators make it clear that the shooter did not commit those crimes because he was secretly gay. But was he homophobic? According to Marczyk, the researchers applied every advantage to the data they were using, to find even spurious relationships that would suggest homophobia or repressed homosexuality.[2]

They broke the data down by men and women; attitudes towards gays, lesbians, and homosexuals in general; those high or low in prejudice; those whose implicit and explicit attractions diverged. No matter how it was sliced, support was not found for the repression idea. When relationships did exist between implicit attraction and explicit attitudes, it usually ran in the opposite direction of the repression

[2] Jesse Marczyk, Ph.D. Homophobia Isn't Repressed Homosexuality.
https://www.psychologytoday.com/us/blog/pop-psych/201608/homophobia-isnt-repressed-homosexuality

hypothesis: those who showed implicit attraction were less negative towards homosexuals (albeit quite modestly).

In short, people's behavior tend to be positive toward those they are attracted to, and negative toward people they hate. A racist who expresses racial hatred doesn't have a repressed desire to belong to the hated race. The racist hates that race! The same is true for those who express hatred toward gay individuals. Therefore, it muddles the issue to label all anti-gay positions as homophobic, automatically implying hatred, because there are those who hate and those who simply disagree. In other words, not all anti-gay perspectives are homophobic.

Still, what was so "grievous" about being gay that God destroyed entire cities to stop it?

# 3 THE ISSUE OF GENDER

The Gay, Lesbian & Straight Education Network (GLSEN) is the "leading national education organization" whose mission is "focused on ensuring safe schools for all students" (www.glsen.org). For more than 25 years, it has reached out to schools and educators to stop the bullying of LGBT students. They have added LGBT-friendly books in school curriculum from kindergarten to 12th grade levels, including the controversial kindergarten book, "Heather Has Two Mommies."

They have also incorporated LGBT-friendly events at schools to increase awareness of homosexual issues, and to foster acceptance of the LGBT lifestyle. For example, in their transgender awareness week, November 14-20, 2015, Gender Terminology 101, GLSEN defined gender as:[3]

A set of cultural identities, expressions and roles – codified as feminine or masculine – that are

[3] GLSEN. Gender terminology 101
https://sites.google.com/bostonpublicschools.org/gsaresources/days-of-action/transgender-awareness-month

assigned to people based upon the interpretation of their bodies, and more specifically, their sexual and reproductive anatomy. Since gender is a social construction, it is possible to reject or modify the gender one is assigned at birth, and to develop, live and express a gender that feels truer and just to oneself.

Gender, according to GLSEN, is merely a social construct that may be accepted, rejected, or modified. Of course, adults can intelligently choose if they agree or disagree with this redefinition of what gender is. But do you believe kindergarten to 12th grade children have the informed capacity to objectively evaluate this indoctrination? It further complicates the matter that GLSEN's campaign disregards parents' position on the topic.

Those who oppose the indoctrination of children to the transgender mindset are labeled intolerant and homophobic. Should parents do otherwise? Doing so would leave children vulnerable to a mindset that produces the highest rates of suicide (more on this later).

Consider Michael Glatze, co-founder of the group, "Young Gay America," and a former writer, editor and passionate advocate for gay rights."[4]  Later, he publicly announced that he was no longer homosexual, and that he believed a gay identity was not in harmony with our created design.  Here are his findings:

> Homosexuality, delivered to young minds, is by its very nature pornographic. It destroys impressionable minds and confuses their developing sexuality; I did not realize this, however, until I was 30 years old… It became clear to me, as I really thought about it – and really prayed about it – that homosexuality prevents us from finding our true self within. We cannot see the truth when we're blinded by homosexuality.

[4] Joseph Nicolosi, Ph.D. CELEBRITIES WHO HAVE LEFT A GAY LIFESTYLE.
https://www.josephnicolosi.com/collection/celebrities-who-have-left-a-gay-lifestyle

Parents, were you aware of this influence upon your kindergarten to 12th grade child? When you prepare their lunch and watch them board the school bus in the mornings, are these the values you wanted them to be taught? And now that you know, what do you plan to do about it?

### Born that way?

There is a school of thought that LGBT orientation is a settled matter. But research conducted by Dr. Lawrence S. Mayer and Dr. Paul R. McHugh, published by The New Atlantis, refutes that conclusion. The following excerpt from their report is presented with their permission.[5]

> This report presents a careful summary and an up-to-date explanation of research—from the biological, psychological, and social sciences—related to sexual orientation and gender identity.

[5] Lawrence S. Mayer, M.B., M.S., Ph.D., Scholar in Residence, Dept. of Psychiatry, Johns Hopkins University School of Medicine & Paul R. McHugh, M.D., Professor of Psychiatry and Behavioral Sciences, Johns Hopkins University School of Medicine. Sexuality and Gender. https://www.thenewatlantis.com/publications/number-50-fall-2016

It is offered in the hope that such an exposition can contribute to our capacity as physicians, scientists, and citizens to address health issues faced by LGBT populations within our society.

## Sexual Orientation

While there is evidence that biological factors such as genes and hormones are associated with sexual behaviors and attractions, there are no compelling causal biological explanations for human sexual orientation. While minor differences in the brain structures and brain activity between homosexual and heterosexual individuals have been identified by researchers, such neurobiological findings do not demonstrate whether these differences are innate; or are the result of environmental and psychological factors.

Longitudinal studies of adolescents suggest that … as many as 80% of male adolescents who report same-sex attractions no longer do so as adults (although the extent to which this figure reflects actual changes in same-sex attractions and not just artifacts of the survey process has been contested by some researchers).

Compared to heterosexuals, non-heterosexuals are about two to three times as likely to have experienced childhood sexual abuse.

## Sexuality, Mental Health Outcomes, and Social Stress

Compared to the general population, non-heterosexual subpopulations are at an elevated risk for a variety of adverse health and mental health outcomes.

Members of the non-heterosexual population are estimated to have about 1.5 times higher risk of experiencing anxiety disorders than members of the heterosexual population, as well as roughly double the risk of depression, 1.5 times the risk of substance abuse, and nearly 2.5 times the risk of suicide.

Members of the transgender population are also at higher risk of a variety of mental health problems compared to members of the non-transgender population. Especially alarmingly, the rate of lifetime suicide attempts across all ages of transgender individuals is estimated at 41%, compared to under 5% in the overall U.S. population.

## Gender Identity

The hypothesis that gender identity is an innate, fixed property of human beings that is independent of biological sex—that a person might be "a man trapped in a woman's body" or "a woman trapped in a man's body"—is not supported by scientific evidence.

According to a recent estimate, about 0.6% of U.S. adults identify as a gender that does not correspond to their biological sex.

Studies comparing the brain structures of transgender and non-transgender individuals have demonstrated weak correlations between brain structure and cross-gender identification. These correlations do not provide any evidence for a neurobiological basis for cross-gender identification.

Compared to the general population, adults who have undergone sex-reassignment surgery continue to have a higher risk of experiencing poor mental health outcomes. One study found that, compared to controls, sex-reassigned individuals were about 5 times more likely to attempt suicide and about 19 times more likely to die by suicide.

What's really happening? Once they've had the gender surgery, the problem worsens dramatically, and they become 19 times more likely to kill themselves. Their psychological health *worsens* after the procedure, but why?

They reject who they are to become what they're told they can be; a promised land that is a lie; only to find themselves in a wilderness of greater confusion, but no closer to achieving this impossible goal. Powerless to return their bodies to its original state, and with no escape in sight, these tortured souls then seek to die. We do not, without profound ignorance or malice, encourage people to take this path.

No man or woman has ever successfully changed his or her gender. Genital mutilations and hormone infusions may modify a person's body, but it can never produce the genuine article. This is why transgender "men" still have babies naturally, and if the surgeon's blade is withheld, transgender "women" still father children biologically: chromosomes remain the same, men remain men, and women remain women. All that the scalpel leaves in its bloody trail are deeper wounds and futile scars. Children are the greatest casualties.

How do we compassionately respond to this tragedy? Is it not to reveal this disorder for the illness that it is, to put an end to the suffering? But in these insane times, that is not the politically correct thing to do! It is easier to follow the earnest mob, parroting loyalty to a cause they never understood, parading their allegiance outside a city in which they would never live, nor wish upon their children; upstanding hypocrites.

Transgender people need professional and empathetic counseling that the gender they were born with is correct; and the church needs to lead in this effort. What have *you* done to make a difference? (We will speak more on this issue in the next chapter). Mayer and McHugh continue.

> Children are a special case when addressing transgender issues. Only a minority of children who experience cross-gender identification will continue to do so into adolescence or adulthood.

> There is little scientific evidence for the therapeutic value of interventions that delay

puberty or modify the secondary sex characteristics of adolescents, although some children may have improved psychological well-being if they are encouraged and supported in their cross-gender identification. There is no evidence that all children who express gender-atypical thoughts or behavior should be encouraged to become transgender.

Gender identification problems were never a part of God's plan for mankind, but He did promise to be there for all people as a helper and an anchor. The question for the LGBT individual is whether or not he or she will seek the Lord and trust in Him, or to continue leaning on secular support that tells them all is well, in an issue where the highest percentages of people seek death as a way out.

It is brutal irony that the LGBT lifestyle is associated with the term "gay" which also means "happy." The pain these souls experience helps clarify why God was so severe toward Sodom and Gomorrah.

# 4  GENDER IDENTITY DISORDER,

## etc.

Psychology Today defines Gender Identity Disorder as, "Strong, persistent feelings of identification with the opposite gender and discomfort with one's own assigned sex that results in significant distress or impairment." It should be noted that they discontinued the term "Gender Identity Disorder" and now identify the condition as, "Gender Dysphoria."

But a dysphoria is "a feeling of being ill at ease," and a disorder is a "lack of order or arrangement; confusion" (Dictionary.com). The implications of each term are significant, which Psychology Today understands, as suggested by their further information on the topic:[6]

> The disturbance can be so pervasive that the mental lives of some individuals revolve only around activities that lessen gender distress. They are often preoccupied with appearance, especially early in the transition to living in the

---

[6] Psychology Today. Gender Dysphoria.
https://www.psychologytoday.com/us/conditions/gender-dysphoria

opposite sex role. Relationships with parents also may be seriously impaired. Some males with gender dysphoria resort to self-treatment with hormones and may (very rarely) perform their own castration or penectomy. Especially in urban centers, some males may engage in prostitution, placing them at a high risk for human immunodeficiency virus (HIV) infection. Suicide attempts and substance-related disorders are common.

This, too, is homophobia.

These are the injured souls who place themselves in kindergarten to 12th grade classrooms and teach children that "gender is a social construct." Why, then, do they kill themselves for living out what they believe? If children learn this gender confusion, are they not at risk?

This fixation with self-destruction is often attributed to social rejection. However, a Gallup Poll of

Americans who support same-sex marriage, as of 15 May 2017, reported that "Sixty-four percent of U.S. adults say same-sex marriages should be recognized by the law as valid… this is the highest percentage to date and continues the generally steady rise since Gallup's trend began in 1996."[7]

On 26 June 2015, a U.S. Supreme Court ruling made same-sex marriage the law of the land, championing the LGBT lifestyle which has now become generally accepted, including by entire denominations of Christian churches. The trend is true even "among members of churches that strongly oppose homosexual relationships as sinful, according to an extensive Pew Research Center survey of U.S. religious beliefs and practices."[8]

The campaign to make homosexuality accepted by the mainstream of society has enjoyed much success;

---

[7] Justin McCarthy. U.S. Support for Gay Marriage Edges to New High.
http://news.gallup.com/poll/210566/support-gay-marriage-edges-new-high.aspx
[8] Carlyle Murphy. Most U.S. Christian groups grow more accepting of homosexuality.
http://www.pewresearch.org/fact-tank/2015/12/18/most-u-s-christian-groups-grow-more-accepting-of-homosexuality/

it is also a campaign that vilifies those who disagree with the LGBT lifestyle. This is creditable to the efforts of Marshall Kirk and Dr. Hunter Madsen.

In 1985 they co-authored "The Gay Agenda," instructing pro-sodomy activists to emphasize the strategic importance of shifting the central issue in the "homosexuality" debate away from "sodomy," toward a sexual pseudo-identity called "gay." By changing the vocabulary, opponents of sodomy were forced into a position where they were seen as attacking the civil rights of "gay" citizens, rather than opposing a specific antisocial behavior.[9] Words shape cultures.

But nature and the scriptures illuminate that moral objection to homosexuality is the healthy position, in spite of social engineering that has conditioned us to think otherwise. Consider this: what is the term for a person who expresses hatred or prejudice against gay, lesbian, bisexual, or transgender people?

[9] Victor J. Adamson. Born Gay Homosexual / Homosexual Agenda Propaganda Exposed! http://www.victorjadamson.com/the-born-gay-hoax-exposed/

Homophobic, right? That was easy.

Now, what is the term for a homosexual person who expresses hatred or prejudice against heterosexual or otherwise non-homosexual people? Bet you don't have a word for that. How about heterophobic? You might even wonder if heterophobia exists, but heterophobic incidents are more common than reported.

For example, a 14-year-old girl and her family were harassed, amidst death threats to her for testifying before the Maryland House that she would like marriage to be between a man and a woman.[10]

A same-sex couple tried to force a baker, Jack Phillips, to make a gay wedding cake for them against his religious beliefs, though there were other cake stores to choose from. The two filed a complaint with the Colorado civil-rights commission against Mr. Philips, who counter-petitioned the Commission. In

---

[10] The New Tolerance Results in Death Threats.
https://www.youtube.com/watch?v=9yvOshGbz9Q

the midst of this, his life was also threatened. The case went to the U.S. Supreme Court which ruled in favor of Mr. Philips, finding that the Commission treated Mr. Phillips with hostility and bias.[11]

Now, what is the term for people with strong feelings against homosexuality on moral or religious grounds, but would do anything to help their homosexual neighbor? The appropriate term is "moralist," or does "homophobic" seem more appealing? If it does, is it because the only word we were ever given was "homophobic," or is it because you believe the notion that all positions against homosexuality is automatically homophobic?

Another Pew Research Center reported that "seven-in-ten now say homosexuality should be accepted by society, compared with just 24% who say it should be discouraged by society ... up 7 percentage points in

---

[11] Nina Totenberg. In Narrow Opinion, Supreme Court Rules For Baker In Gay-Rights Case. https://www.npr.org/2018/06/04/605003519/supreme-court-decides-in-favor-of-baker-over-same-sex-couple-in-cake-shop-case

the past year, and up 19 points from 11 years ago."[12]

Clearly, the social rejection argument for the extreme rates of transgender suicide is not supported by the facts. Sadly, the self-hate that drives them to mutilate their bodies, also drives them to self-destruction. The solution cannot be to celebrate this as natural, any more than it would be to celebrate an open wound as natural.

A man was meant for a woman, and a woman for a man. As God instructed, "That is why a man leaves his father and mother and is united to his wife, and they become one flesh" (Genesis 2:24).

But this presents a paradox.

People need to love and be loved. However, the fires that ignite our sexual passions are not sparked by scriptures. Arguably, "genuine love" is the prevailing

---

[12] Pew Research Center. Homosexuality, gender and religion. http://www.people-press.org/2017/10/05/5-homosexuality-gender-and-religion/#changing-views-on-acceptance-of-homosexuality

standard for intimate relationships. It meets our human need for affection. Paradoxically, the remedy creates the problem.

There is tension between our sexual choices and the biblical principles that tell us some of them are wrong. And cultural norms have changed. Millions now ask, "What could be wrong with two people in a relationship of 'genuine love' for each other? So what, if they happen to be gay?"

# 5   GAY LOVE AND THE CHURCH

Sexual union impacts the entire person: body, soul, and spirit. Therefore, when consummated sinfully, it corrupts completely, and therein lies the problem. For example, if we applied the "genuine love" criteria to pedophilia, most of us will agree, it could not survive close scrutiny.

The North American Man/Boy Love Association (NAMBLA) is a gay group that advocates for pedophile sex between grown men and boys. Their site celebrates incidents of gay pedophilia, such as "'Molested' and Glad," where a man relates that his first sexual experience was a gay relationship he had when he was 13 years old, with a man he believed to have been in his 30's. This molestation, which he continues to view as a positive experience, reinforced his homosexual inclinations as a child, and he grew up to be a gay adult.[13]

NAMBLA argues that their pedophile relationships are healthy, because of love and commitment. Adults

---

[13] Brian. Personal Experience/Stories of Man/Boy Love.
https://www.nambla.org/mglad.html

in consenting incestuous relationships make the same argument, as do spouses who consent to an open marriage. Who can say whether they are right or wrong? This shines light on a need for an objective standard that is higher than our personal values.

The truth that the Creator Himself is love (1 John 4:8) presents another truth: His standard is the most accurate for measuring love. Sincerity and commitment cannot negate God's instructions against homosexuality, in the same context that it cannot sanctify the vileness of pedophilia, incest, or adultery. Can love be evil? Yes! Whenever sin is involved. Hence, the suggestion that love and commitment would sanctify homosexual unions falls epically short.

Love does not dishonor. It protects, including the vulnerability of children. It is not self-seeking but unselfishly looks out for the best of everyone. Therefore, love neither lives a life of willful sin, nor encourages others to do so, because sin begets the ultimate penalty: eternal damnation.

Love endeavors never to behave in a manner inconsistent with God's scriptural guidance, but delights and rejoices in obeying His word, which is God's very Truth (John 17:17). It is always undergirded by the spiritual and emotional security of God's sure foundation, and functions from a reciprocal position of protection, trust, and hope. Consequently, love always perseveres.

This is the love that the scriptures teach, illuminated in 1 Corinthians 13. It is the love God freely offers to everyone who asks, but it must be received on His terms, which is a committed relationship to follow and obey Christ, based on the truth He has revealed in the scriptures. Homosexual intimacy is sin.

The severity with which God dealt with Sodom and Gomorrah is a warning for our times. But insulated by thousands of years from the harshness of this judgment, people now struggle with that warning.

And so, we ask, why?

God has never explained. He only pointed us to the tremendous eternal consequences. Isn't that enough? Unlike other sins where He simply drew a line, here, He took away reasonable doubt and implored us with love to trust and obey.

We may never fully understand God's values, but it is most unwise to place yourself opposite a line that He has drawn. That line is, sexual intimacy and marriage must be between a man and a woman.

But even churches now ask, why?

## Marriage and Same-Sex Unions

Some churches teach that the love and commitment between same-sex partners, many of whom have been together for decades, justifies marriage as the reasonable next step. Consider the following scenarios as we examine "love and commitment" as the standard for marriage.

Charles and Kathy are madly in love. It took a little flirting at first, for him to win her heart, but for Charles, it was love at first sight. Eventually, she learned to love the intimacy and security he offered her. She felt safe with him. Their relationship blossomed until they consummated their passions in Charles' bedroom.

However, Charles dares not let their love be more than their little secret. You see, Charles is a grown man, and Kathy is eleven years old. One day, summoning up enough courage, Charles approached pastor Paul to ask him to marry them. After getting over the shock, the pastor asks Charles, "What could you possibly want with this child?" Charles' answer was simple, "We love each other."

If this was your child, would love justify giving her to Charles in marriage? Of course not! If the story was about Charles and a boy named Ken, or his daughter Sara, or his son John, would your answer be any different? Again, of course not!

A moral person would agree that "love and commitment" was no justification for those vile relationships, and that the victim needed protection from this sexual predator! But *why?* Shouldn't "love and commitment" have made these children safe, as NAMBLA and others would argue?

While the "love and commitment" fallacy is easy to see when the issue involves children and other vulnerable people, it gets cloudy when it involves adults. This is because their informed consent suggests that their behavior is sound.

For example, being a patient man, Charles waits and decides to marry Ken when he is 21. Like the molested boy mentioned by NAMBLA, Ken agrees to the marriage because he believes his experience was healthy. Here, in addition to "love and commitment," there is now informed consent by two adults. What could be wrong with this? Some would say, nothing. After all, they love and are committed to each other, and are consenting adults. But God's standard has never changed.

> Or do you not know that wrongdoers will not
> inherit the kingdom of God? Do not be
> deceived: Neither the sexually immoral, nor
> idolaters, nor adulterers, nor men who have sex
> with men, nor thieves, nor the greedy, nor
> drunkards, nor slanderers, nor swindlers, will
> inherit the kingdom of God (1 Corinthians 6:9-
> 11).

"Love and commitment" can never purify a sinful relationship. Similarly, because sin violates God's will for mankind, marriage can never sanctify an LGBT union. No church by-laws or Supreme Court ruling can change that truth. Jesus said, "Whoever comes to me I will never drive away" (John 6:37). Many have answered God's call and given their lives to Christ, in their struggle against homosexual inclinations. Still, can a Christian be gay? This question has divided entire church denominations.

Most churches abide by fundamental biblical principles that forbid same-sex relationships. But the following have adopted a different approach.

### The Episcopal Church

In 1976, the General Convention of the Episcopal Church declared that "homosexual persons are children of God who have a full and equal claim with all other persons upon the love, acceptance, and pastoral concern and care of the Church" (1976-A069). Since then, faithful Episcopalians have been working toward a greater understanding and radical inclusion of all of God's children.

Along the way, The Episcopal Church has garnered a lot of attention, but with the help of organizations such as Integrity USA, the church has continued its work toward full inclusion of lesbian, gay, bisexual, and transgender (LGBT) Episcopalians. In 2003, the first openly gay bishop was consecrated; in 2009, General

Convention resolved that God's call is open to all; in 2012, a provisional rite of blessing for same-gender relationships was authorized, and discrimination against transgender persons in the ordination process was officially prohibited; and in 2015, the canons of the church were changed to make the rite of marriage available to all people, regardless of gender.

To our lesbian, gay, bisexual, and transgender brothers and sisters: "The Episcopal Church welcomes you!"[14]

## The Presbyterian Church

Persons in a same-gender relationship may be considered for ordination and/or installation as deacons, ruling elders, and teaching elders (ministers of the Word and Sacrament) within the PC (USA).

---

[14] The Episcopal Church. Who We Are. http://www.episcopalchurch.org/page/lgbt-church

Ordaining bodies (sessions and presbyteries) are permitted but not required to ordain lesbian, gay, bisexual, or transgender persons. Candidates for ordination and/or installation must be considered as individuals on a case-by-case basis; it is not permissible to establish a policy that excludes a category of persons in the abstract.

Pastors are permitted but not required to officiate at any wedding, including same-sex weddings, based either on conscience or the pastor's discernment of the couple's readiness to take on the responsibilities of marriage.

Sessions are permitted but not required to authorize use of the church's property for a wedding, including same-sex weddings, for reasons of conscience or other reasons.[15]

---

[15] Presbyterian Church (U.S.A.). Sexuality and Same-Gender Relationships.
https://www.presbyterianmission.org/what-we-believe/social-issues/sexuality/

## The United Church of Christ

THEREFORE LET IT BE RESOLVED, that the Twenty-fifth General Synod of the United Church of Christ affirms equal marriage rights for couples regardless of gender and declares that the government should not interfere with couples regardless of gender who choose to marry and share fully and equally in the rights, responsibilities and commitment of legally recognized marriage; and

LET IT BE FURTHER RESOLVED, that the Officers of the United Church of Christ are called upon to communicate this resolution to local, state and national legislators, urging them to support equal marriage rights for couples regardless of gender.[16]

By sanctioning the LGBT lifestyle and ordaining LGBT individuals, these churches have literally taken

---

[16] United Church of Christ. Equal Marriage Rights for All [PDF], Adopted at the Twenty-fifth General Synod on July 4, 2005. http://uccfiles.com/pdf/2005-EQUAL-MARRIAGE-RIGHTS-FOR-ALL.pdf

homosexuality from the closet to the pulpit. But let *this* be resolved: the sanction of sin by any church can never cancel the darkness it brings upon the soul. God's guidance remains remain clear.

> Do not have sexual relations with a man as one does with a woman; that is detestable... Everyone who does any of these detestable things—such persons must be cut off from their people (Leviticus 18:22, 29).

> Because of this, God gave them over to shameful lusts. Even their women exchanged natural sexual relations for unnatural ones. In the same way the men also abandoned natural relations with women and were inflamed with lust for one another. Men committed shameful acts with other men, and received in themselves the due penalty for their error (Romans 1:26-28).

God drew a line in the sand: His unequivocal voice against homosexuality. That matters. For when we breathe the final sigh, and our spirit returns to the Creator, the one question we dare not miss is, by whose standard did you live; yours or mine? Disobedience and obedience are entirely our choice, each leading to opposite consequences. Choose God and forsake sin. It's the right choice.

## The Problem that Sin Created

Sin separates God's creation from Him and, therefore, God hates sin. "As I live," God swears, "I have no pleasure in the death of the wicked, but that the wicked turn from his way and live" (Ezekiel 33:11). But God is also a Judge. His judgment against Sodom and Gomorrah was against the sin of homosexuality, not because He hated its residents.

It was no coincidence that the first thing He said in the scriptures was, "Let there be light," which represents righteousness chasing away the darkness of sin (Genesis 1:3). Then He made that separation the permanent reality we know as light and darkness, day and night.

This is a picture of the absolute futility of living in sin while professing to serve God. It also depicts the blessedness of Jesus' sacrifice because, in Jesus' radiance, God sees His own Light in us, the only acceptable standard of righteousness.[17] To believe in God is to turn away from sin and walk in His light (1 John 1:6-7).

Can a gay person who has chosen to serve Christ continue to practice the same-sex lifestyle without spiritual compromise? Clearly, no. A Christian may find himself (or herself) struggling against same-sex temptations, while trying to serve God faithfully. As with struggles against any other sin, that Christian's faithfulness to God in the midst of these challenges will be rewarded. But those who give in to these lusts are living in sin. Hence, a Christian may be challenged by gay issues, but a gay Christian—a person who professes faith in Christ while living a homosexual lifestyle—is an oxymoron.

---

[17] See 2 Corinthians 5:21 and Isaiah 64:6

## Sin, the Enemy Within

What then is sin, and why does God take such an extreme position against it, for He said, "The one who sins is the one who will die" (Ezekiel 18:4)? The Hebrew word for sin in that scripture is *chata*, which means to miss the mark, in the sense of going astray.

The word sin in Romans 6:23, "For the wages of sin is death," is the Greek word *hamartia*, and also means to go astray. This concept informs our understanding of the English word "transgress" which means, "To violate a law, command, moral code, etc." (Dictionary.com). To sin is to go astray from God's path for our lives, but why does this kill us spiritually?

It is impossible to go "from" without also going "toward." When we go *from* God, we simultaneously go *toward* sin. In Romans 6:23, the Bible describes this departure from God as a redirection toward death, and here is why: God is light; in Him there is no darkness at all (1 John 1:5).

All life forms need light in order to live. This is true both in the natural and in the spiritual realms. It is also why Lucifer and his followers became creatures of darkness, devoid of life, when they were exiled from the light of God's Presence.

To turn away from God is to orient yourself away from light, toward darkness and death. The fact that Satan is completely sinful is equivalent to the truth that he also has no light at all in him, hence, his constant companion is death. Spiritually speaking, our sinful nature killed us too. That being the case, how does a Christian with same-sex orientation deal with the issue of sin while trying to serve God?

# 6  SEXUAL ORIENTATION

What's your sexual orientation? According to Dictionary.com, "orientation" is, "The ability to locate oneself in one's environment with reference to time, place, and people." The root word, "orient," means, "To place in any definite position with reference to the points of the compass or other locations" (Dictionary.com). Therefore, an orientation is simply where you are on a given issue, or in a given place. In terms of sexual orientation, it is generally defined as where your sexual interests are, regarding one gender versus another.

Our physical construct and nature itself prove that God designed sexual intercourse for two people, male and female, perfectly complementing each other for pleasure and procreation. Since this is God's construct, it is the natural way of things, as well as the standard for normal. Blindness, deafness, and other maladies also occur naturally, but we agree that they are unhealthy states, and therefore, not normal. Similarly, the current argument that homosexuality is natural and therefore normal is unsound, because it violates God's intention for human sexual relations.

Anything outside of the Creator's plan strays from the right path; it is a ship on a vast ocean, oriented toward the west, when home is to the north. As long as it continues in its westward orientation it will never reach home. The final outcome for a soul that continues on a sinful path is to be lost throughout eternity. While healing from same-sex orientation is possible, like a ship at sea, it is a route often defined by determination and turbulence. But God's way is the only way home, and Christians are charged to be the lighthouse of Christ to help others make it to safety.

## Yes, There's a Way Out

The American Psychiatric Association (APA) doubts that people can change from same-sex orientation.[18] Interestingly, the first formal protest against the APA, conducted May 22, 1994, in Philadelphia, was by a

---

[18] American Psychological Association. What about therapy intended to change sexual orientation from gay to straight? http://www.apa.org/topics/lgbt/orientation.aspx

---

group of people who reported that they had substantially changed their sexual orientation, and that change is possible for others. A similar demonstration occurred at the 2000 APA convention in Chicago, then again at their 2006 Convention in New Orleans.[19] People do change from same-sex orientation.

A beautiful gem of hope nestles amidst the exclamations that pronounce God's judgment against homosexuality. By now we are familiar with scriptures like, "Do not be deceived: Neither the sexually immoral, nor idolaters, nor adulterers, nor men who have sex with men, nor thieves ... will inherit the kingdom of God" (1 Corinthians 6:9-10). But have you considered what follows, in verse 11? "And that is what some of you were. But you were washed, you were sanctified, you were justified in the name of the Lord Jesus Christ and by the Spirit of our God."

[19] Truth According to Scripture. NARTH's Response to the APA Claims on Homosexuality. https://www.truthaccordingtoscripture.com/documents/politics/narth.php#.Wv9IRUgvyUk

"And that is what some of you *were*"! This is biblical affirmation that change is possible. What brings about the change? When we come to Jesus, He washes us, sanctifies us, and justifies us through His Holy Spirit. We are made holy, pure, and righteous; as fully accepted as one of the apostles. This cleansing process is what every person experiences after he or she welcomes Jesus into his or her life.

For the soul that discovers this truth, the words of Paul may never have sounded more glorious: "Therefore, if anyone is in Christ, he is a new creation; old things have passed away; behold, all things have become new" (2 Corinthians 5:17, NKJV). Spiritually speaking, we become a new person because the change in us is so complete.

For every transformed person, as you scale your mountain of victory, be prepared for a peculiar discovery when you reach the top. You will find many others already there, long before you arrived; people just like you, who also realized that they, too, could change.

Based on research by Dr. Joseph Nicolosi, the following public figures are among countless others who have turned away from a gay lifestyle and are now happily enjoying heterosexual relationships.[20]

## Jan Clausen

Clausen is the author of a dozen books in various genres. Her poetry and creative prose are widely published in journals and anthologies. Nicolosi provided the following quote, with reference to Clausen's experience while gay.

After 12 years in a lesbian marriage, Jan Clausen fell in love with a man. Since her identities as writer and lesbian were intertwined, all hell broke loose. Clausen's books are yanked off college reading lists. She loses friends, community, and status.

[20] Joseph Nicolosi, Ph.D. CELEBRITIES WHO HAVE LEFT A GAY LIFESTYLE.
https://www.josephnicolosi.com/collection/celebrities-who-have-left-a-gay-lifestyle

Contradicting the idea that people are born gay, Clausen said the following, as reported by Nicolosi.

> What's got to stop is the rigging of history to make the 'either/or' look permanent and universal. I understand why this argument may sound erotic to outsiders for whom the public assertion of a coherent, unchanging lesbian or gay identity has proved an indispensable tactic in the battle against homophobic persecution.

Nicolosi continued, "Later, Clausen quotes the popular lesbian poet Audre Lorde, who admits the untruths associated with the 'born gay' idea, when she writes, 'I do not believe our wants have made all our lies holy.'"

### Bob Dixon

Sen. Bob Dixon is an American Republican politician who was first elected to the Missouri House of Representatives in 2002 and served four terms. Between 2004 and 2008 he served as Majority Caucus

Chairman and chaired the House Transportation committee.

Mr. Dixon said that abuses he suffered as a child, and consequent confusion as a teenager, were the incidents that caused him to engage in gay relationships. His campaign issued a statement affirming his faith in God and support for traditional marriage. Dr. Nicolosi provided the following statements by Mr. Dixon.

'Through the years, I have publicly spoken about being abused as a child and the confusion this caused me as a teenager,' said Dixon in the statement. 'There are literally thousands of Missourians who will understand how heartbreaking childhood abuse can be -- though few might be willing to acknowledge it.'

'I have put the childhood abuse, and the teenage confusion behind me,' said Dixon, who has a wife and three children. 'What others intended for harm has resulted in untold good. I have overcome, and will not allow evil to win.'

### Jessica Ellen Cornish (Jessie J)

Jessie J, an English singer and songwriter, is the first British female artist to have six top ten singles from a studio album. Her third album, "Sweet Talker," was preceded by the single, "Bang Bang," which debuted at number one in the UK and went multi-platinum worldwide. She has sold over 20 million singles and 3 million albums worldwide, as of January 2015.

An associate, Chloe Govan, once said, "Jessie might have been with boys in the past — but she is 100 per cent gay. Jessie was openly lesbian and didn't hide it." In an interview about her previous life as a lesbian, Jessie said the following.

> Passing comments [were] made into 'facts' that [people] can never change. Guess what? They can change. As they should. And I have changed and grown up ALOT, and that's allowed. And I

feel more comfortable in my own skin now than ever before. We all are on a journey and I refuse to feel boxed and judged because of how I felt once! A long-ass time ago. Vegetarians eat meat sometimes. Get it? People change.

### Dennis Jernigan

Dennis Jernigan, an Oklahoma native, is a singer and songwriter of contemporary Christian music. Here is Mr. Jernigan's insight on his transformed life.

This statement will probably produce a lot of controversy, but this is how I think of myself: I do not consider myself a recovering/former/ex gay. I consider myself a new creation. The slate of my mind is being erased and the old thoughts are being replaced with new thinking. What I have discovered in the process is that when I change my thoughts, my attitudes change. When I change my attitudes, my behaviors change. When I change my behaviors, my perspectives change. When my perspectives change, I see life from a vantage point that homosexuality NEVER afforded me.

Being gay is not a permanent state. With commitment and determination, it is entirely possible to renounce the gay lifestyle for a heterosexual life, as we've just seen. The power of God is there to assist anyone who asks.

God tells us that if we confess our sins, He is faithful and just and will forgive us our sins and purify us from all unrighteousness (1 John 1:9). Knowing that we were are all born broken because of sin, and that we each have challenges we need to overcome, He provided this "out," so whenever we fail, we can obtain forgiveness, mercy, and strength. With determination and prayer, we can all eventually overcome our weaknesses.

For everyone who decides to follow Christ, a transformation happens. "Therefore, there is now no condemnation for those who are in Christ Jesus, because through Christ Jesus the law of the Spirit who gives life has set you free from the law of sin and death" (Romans 8:1-2). However, the Christian journey is designed to be taken one day at a time, one step at a time, one small victory at a time.

Victory will come by first recognizing and acknowledging that the LGBT lifestyle is sinful. Without this first step, God's light cannot gain the entrance it needs to break down the remaining barriers. Once sin has been acknowledged, this must be followed by repentance, which means deciding to turn away from sin and asking God for forgiveness. In many cases, these simple steps are all it takes. Through prayer, fasting, and determination, people are able to live as God intended for them. For others, however, confession and repentance are only the beginning of the process.

### At the Root of the Matter

As with all persistent sins, there is a spiritual component that empowers homosexuality, deeply rooted in the core of the person's being. In these cases, prayer and fasting must be accompanied by direct spiritual intervention and follow-up. For example, here is a case where prayers unaccompanied by fasting would have proved insufficient (Matthew 17:14-16, and 18-21, NKJV).

> And when they had come to the multitude, a man came to Him, kneeling down to Him and saying, 'Lord, have mercy on my son, for he is an epileptic and suffers severely; for he often falls into the fire and often into the water.

> 'So I brought him to Your disciples, but they could not cure him.' … And Jesus rebuked the demon, and it came out of him; and the child was cured from that very hour. Then the disciples came to Jesus privately and said, 'Why could we not cast it out?'

> So Jesus said to them, 'Because of your unbelief; for assuredly, I say to you, if you have faith as a

mustard seed, you will say to this mountain, 'Move from here to there,' and it will move; and nothing will be impossible for you. However, this kind does not go out except by prayer and fasting.'

It is essential to pray and fast in dealing with the spiritual aspect of homosexuality. And it may at times be necessary to cast out an evil spirit, as we saw in the example. Everyone's need is different. Some cases will require more intense spiritual intervention than others, but the church of God is powerful.

The weapons we fight with are not the weapons of the world. On the contrary, they have divine power to demolish strongholds. We demolish arguments and every pretension that sets itself up against the knowledge of God, and we take captive every thought to make it obedient to Christ (2 Corinthians 10:4-5).

The process of taking up God's authority against

homosexuality and the spiritual entities that empower it is called spiritual warfare. It is vital to seek help and support from trusted leaders in the church, who understand spiritual warfare, and are sensitive to the problem.

Pentecostal churches tend to be more explicit in this area of ministry, however, every Christian and every church is equipped by God to assist. That said, due diligence is necessary because all churches are not equally comfortable with the subject.

Directly ask if they understand the need for spiritual warfare and if they have experience in helping people in this manner. Additionally, find out if the church has a track record of successful, confidential support to others who have sought their assistance? If you cannot find this level of trust and spiritual assistance in the church you are currently attending, reach out to a different Christian church where you can find it.

The highest mandate for any Christian church is to

love and selflessly meet the needs of others. In fact, love and compassion is the standard all Christians are measured by, to the extent that Christ told His disciples, "By this everyone will know that you are my disciples, if you love one another" (John 13:35). A church that abides by the teachings of the Bible is a safe place to be, because of this fundamental requirement to love.

Sadly, in the noisy demands for political correctness, some churches have adopted a loose interpretation of the scriptural mandate against homosexuality, as we already saw. Before baring your soul to any minister, find out what their position is. Is it consistent with the fact that God declares homosexuality a sin? Does their ministry follow the Christian ideals of love, integrity, trust, and accountability?

One quick way of knowing is by reading their "Statements of Faith" (usually available on their website) and other literature about the church. Many churches are transparent about their position on same-sex issues; stay away from the ones that do not abide by God's standards.

## Intersex Challenges

In rare cases, some people are born with male and female sexual organs, an anomaly defined as intersex. It ranges from having both male and female organs present, to having external genitalia different from internal sexual organs; or having ambiguous internal and/or external sexual organs. Hormonal levels may also be inconsistent with that of the more developed external genitalia, resulting in sexual confusion.

Adult individuals often reject the gender chosen for them in childhood, in preference of the gender they more closely identify with. For example, individuals with ambiguous external genitalia but a fairly developed phallus tend to be reared as males, however, during puberty, they sometimes develop breasts and may even menstruate. Parents now wait until later in life when an informed decision can be made by the intersex person.

In order to discover an intersex baby's true gender, specialists perform tests such as chromosome analysis, blood tests, and exploratory surgery. Treatment for adults includes surgery to reinforce the chosen gender, accompanied by hormonal therapy. But psychological and emotional hurdles often persist, even after treatment. Loving support and understanding is essential in helping intersex persons through the difficulties they inevitably encounter.

Caster Semenya, who represented South Africa in the 2009 Olympics as a female, is one of the more famous intersex individuals. Her high levels of testosterone, evidenced by distinctively male characteristics, brought her gender into question. The governing body of the Olympics launched an investigation and her condition was made public.

The intersex person's gender choice is driven by a need for self-identity. They may use sexual orientation as a tool for answering the question, "Am I male or female?" This is not the same question as,

"Why am I sexually attracted to people of my own gender?" which indicates knowledge of one's own gender.

LGBT individuals may describe themselves as having their true gender trapped in the body of the opposite sex, therefore having a "same-sex" preference. But we saw that eighty percent of males who reported homosexual or bisexual feelings as children later identified exclusively as heterosexual. We also saw that everyone can change.

Transgender individuals reject he/she gender labels, yet, if a man who became transgender is attracted to another man, he defends this as a he/she attraction. And as we learned, the inner turmoil that accompanies the transgender experience often leads to devastating outcomes.

In the midst of the turbulence of these souls, the only refuge remains, His arms outstretched. Recall Jesus' promise, "Whoever comes to me I will never drive away" (John 6:37).

Help is available for everyone who wishes to overcome same-sex attraction.

# 7 THERE ARE MANY RESOURCES

No one walks this world alone, unless they choose to. The Christian ministries listed below are among many that offer counseling and assistance on various challenges of life, including how to overcome same-sex attraction. The following information is based on an online search and is provided for information purposes. No relationship, sponsorship, or endorsement exists between this author and any of these agencies. The reader is required to exercise his or her own due diligence before deciding whether or not to work with any of these agencies.

## Living Hope Ministries[21]

Children are among our most vulnerable, because they lack the maturity and experience required to make informed decisions. Living Hope Ministries offer "a safe place for individuals seeking restoration and healing through weekly support group meetings, moderated online support forums, in-depth discipleship programs, and active partnerships with

---

[21] Living Hope Ministries. https://www.livehope.org/about-us/who-we-are/

churches around the world." It includes an outreach to children experiencing gender related challenges. Their website (listed in the footnote) has more information.

## Christian Counselor Directory[22]

The Christian Counselor Directory offers "a comprehensive listing of Professional and Pastoral therapists who aspire to strong principals, ethics, and Christian faith." They seek psychological and spiritual wholeness for their clients, with the aid of "either a board certified or state licensed professional or pastoral therapist who has earned at least a graduate degree in counseling, psychology, or related field." The therapy seeker is asked to review the credentials and specialties of the counselors in their directory and choose one that best fits their needs.

## Reconciliation Ministries[23]

Reconciliation Ministries offers private pastoral

---

[22] Christian Counselor Directory. https://www.christiancounselordirectory.com/
[23] Reconciliation Ministries. http://www.recmin.org/counseling/

counseling and licensed professional counseling for those struggling with sexual and relational brokenness, and for their family members. They feature Christ-centered counseling with a strong emphasis on healing prayer, allowing the Holy Spirit to minister to the wounds and misconceptions that cause pain and leave one open to sexual sin. They also provide internet and telephone-based counseling to missionaries and other individuals serving overseas who do not otherwise have access to pastoral care.

## First Stone Ministries[24]

First Stone's primary purpose is to lead the sexually and relationally broken into a liberating relationship with Jesus Christ as Savior and Lord. Discipleship and restoration in every area of one's life is stressed; however, there is detailed emphasis on overcoming all forms of sexual brokenness including homosexuality, sexual abuse and addiction to pornography.

---

[24] First Stone Ministries. http://www.firststone.org/

---

These are just a few of the many resources available. Everyone does not experience change at the same pace, but everyone can experience change that with persistence, will produce the desired objective. LGBT individuals can look to God with hope, because He is faithful, and is able to meet all their needs. But this is not a journey of quick fixes. Like all worthwhile endeavors, it will require commitment and sacrifice, in spite of the intermittent failures that are bound to happen along the way.

As we target unwanted behavior patterns for change, we build foundations that reinforce desired behaviors. The Twelve Step Program of Alcoholics Anonymous[25] is a proven model with decades of history to its credit at helping people in their struggles to overcome compelling behaviors. The following twelve steps was adapted from that model.

[25] Lauren Brande. About the Alcoholics Anonymous (AA) 12-Step Recovery Program. https://www.recovery.org/topics/alcoholics-anonymous-12-step/

## A Twelve-Step Approach

**Step 1: Admit you are powerless on your own, and that your life has become unmanageable.**

This first step begins the process and is the most important. It unmasks the lie that we are self-sufficient and reveals a very real, human person who needs help.

**Step 2: Come to believe that a Power greater than your own can restore you to wholeness.**

That Power is Almighty God who calls you into a loving relationship of commitment and trust in Him. It is difficult to succeed by your own power, but through Christ, and with fellow Christians supporting you, you can succeed.

**Step 3: Make a decision to turn your life over to the care of God.**

If you have not yet done so, commit your life to Jesus as your Lord and Savior. Power to overcome temptation is a part of the blessings that comes with salvation. You can commit your life to Jesus by (1) prayerfully admitting that you are a sinner, (2) asking God to forgive your sins, (3) asking Jesus to become the Lord of your life, and (4) committing to serve God by obeying His principles, as found in the Bible. Take the time now to pray and commit your life to Jesus. Once you've done this, it is vitally important that you join a church and receive the support you will need as a new believer in Jesus. For details, refer to "The Romans Road" in Chapter 8.

**Step 4: Make a searching and fearless moral inventory of yourself.**

Come to terms with where you are in your struggle against same-sex attraction or transgenderism. For example, did these drives result from abuse you suffered as a child (knowing the root cause can make a difference)? Are there any issues that you believe might prevent you from succeeding in this effort? In which areas are you strongest and weakest? Be honest with yourself. This is necessary for determining where your strengths and weaknesses are, including where you most need to reach out for help, such as from your pastor or one of the ministries identified earlier.

## Step 5: Admit to God, to yourself, and to another human being the exact nature of your needs.

The scriptures say, "If we confess our sins, He is faithful and just and will forgive us our sins and purify us from all unrighteousness" (1 John 1:9). This scary but liberating step creates accountability within ourselves and with God. Seek the help of trusted leaders in your church and let them hold you accountable. That said, do not feel forced to do anything before you are fully ready. Always pray for God's guidance, then trust that He will help you.

## Step 6: Be entirely ready to accept God's solution.

You truly do have the power to succeed, but victory over past habits may come only after a battle. Be ready to accept change in your lifestyle. Study your bible, learn God's principles and apply them to your life.

Some of these principles will conflict with your previous beliefs. These are the areas where change is most needed; where the greatest struggles and growth will likely happen. Your commitment to follow Christ will help anchor you. In the midst of your challenges, remember God has promised, "Never will I leave you; never will I forsake you" (Hebrews 13:5).

## Step 7: Humbly ask God for strength to overcome your shortcomings.

God responds to the humble heart that cries out to Him. As you humble yourself to God and request that He heals you completely, trust and expect Him to do so, and stay the course! God will prove Himself true and faithful.

## Step 8: Make a list of all persons you have harmed and be willing to make amends.

Let the scriptures and your conscience be your guide. Understand that in some cases, where you may have offended someone, the most you will be able to do is ask for their forgiveness and admit to them you were wrong. In other cases, such as where hostility exists, it may be best to keep things at a distance. Here, your support team at church can be an invaluable source for biblical guidance.

**Step 9: Make direct amends to such people wherever possible, except when doing so would injure you, them, or others**.

This relates to the steps you took in #8.

**Step 10: Continue to take personal inventory and when you are wrong, promptly admit it.**

Again, discipline and determination are vital for success. Confess your failures to your team for accountability purposes, repent to God, and reaffirm your resolve to be victorious over transgenderism and same-sex attraction. Every effort brings you closer to the mark of attaining God's best for your life. He will give you the strength you need.

**Step 11: Pray, fast, and meditate on God's word to improve your knowledge of God, your**

**relationship with Him, and to increase your power to overcome**.

Prayer, fasting, and meditating on God's word changes our mindset. This is a key weapon in combating ungodly urges because it helps to conform the mind to the will of God, and to effect the change we need.

**Step 12: Having had a spiritual awakening, stand in support of God's principles, and practice God's laws in all your affairs.**

Make a stand for Jesus. You may lose some friends along the way, but they will be replaced by new ones. You may become lonely, but through a relationship with Christ, through prayer, you will discover the joy of God's presence in your life. You may experience the pain of giving up something that has meant a lot to you, but there is no price equal to the blessing of God upon your life, culminated by eternity in heaven with Jesus. *The best is still ahead!*

# 8  CHOOSE JESUS!

Jesus said, "I have come that they may have life, and that they may have it more abundantly" (John 10:10, NKJV). Here is a glimpse of what that means: "Eye has not seen, nor ear heard, nor have entered into the heart of man the things which God has prepared for those who love Him" (1 Corinthians 2:9, NKJV). People walk on streets made of gold in heaven (Revelation 21:21). Thus, the standard for wealth on earth is something God gives us to walk upon.

What then are the precious things in our future home, so resplendent in glory that our collective imagination cannot perceive it? Wonders that surpass our deepest yearnings can never be captured by words. But the Spirit of the Lord invites us to be a part of the family of Christ, and a partaker of this Blessed Hope. Will you ignore God's call?

Heaven is worth far more than any sacrifice you will ever make on earth. Jesus paved the path by laying down His own life on the cross, just for you. Now it's your turn to lay down your life for Him.

Renounce the LGBT lifestyle and choose Jesus!

## The Romans Road

*God Loves You!*

For God so loved the world that He gave His only begotten Son, that whoever believes in Him should not perish but have everlasting life (John 3:16, NKJV). This includes all people of all social or spiritual or sexual orientations. It includes *you!*

*God's wants you to have abundant life!*

Jesus said, "I have come that they may have life, and that they may have it more abundantly" (John 10:10, NKJV).

*But sin created a problem*

Sin separated us from fellowship with God, because all have sinned and fall short of the glory of God (Romans 3:23, NKJV).

*The Penalty for our sin is death.*

For the wages of sin is death, but the gift of God is

eternal life in Christ Jesus our Lord (Romans 6:23, NKJV).

### *Jesus paid the penalty for our sin!*

But God demonstrates His own love toward us, in that while we were yet sinners, Christ died for us (Romans 5:8, NKJV).

### *The great opportunity this created*

And now, "whoever calls on the name of the Lord shall be saved" (Romans 10:13, NKJV).

### *How to become saved*

If you confess with your mouth the Lord Jesus, and believe in your heart that God has raised Him from the dead, you will be saved. For with the heart one believes unto righteousness, and with the mouth confession is made unto salvation (Romans 10:9-10, NKJV).

### *What to do now*

Pray with me: *"Lord Jesus, I am a sinner. Forgive me and*

*save my soul. I acknowledge that the LGBT lifestyle is sin. I turn away from my sinful ways and commit myself, from now on, to serve you for the rest of my life. I commit to reading the Bible to learn and obey your principles, and to develop a lifestyle of prayer for strength to remain faithful in times of temptation. Jesus, thank You for saving my soul, and for the wonderful things you have in store for me. Amen!"*

Congratulations on making this very important step! The last step is to become baptized *because* you are saved. This serves as a public confession of your belief in Christ and is something God requires of all new believers. Find a church to attend regularly and ask your pastor for more information about becoming baptized.

*Welcome to the family of Christ!*

## Make a Difference

It is better to light one candle than to curse the darkness. Those immortal words of William L. Watkinson, since 1907, still compel us today. It is easy to feel engaged, while complaining about the changes that need to happen, as we watch things continue to get worse. Having voiced our concerns, sometimes loudly, perhaps we feel like we've done enough.

But millions of people still believe there is no eternal consequence to being LGBT. Millions more simply don't care. You have read this far because you care. The ultimate concern has never been about whether or not being LGBT makes a person more or less successful as a human being.

As a matter of fact, your LGBT neighbor is likely to be a law-abiding, tax paying citizen who contributes to society. But God destroyed Sodom and Gomorrah because of sin. In the midst of the political correctness that clouds the spiritual consequences of sin, souls are still being lost. You were charged in the Great Commission to win souls! Let the information you learned in this book be *your* light in the darkness. Don't just keep it to yourself!

Thanks for taking the time to learn more about God's heart for people: to save souls from sin! Jesus said, "The harvest truly is plentiful, but the laborers are few" (Matthew 9:37). Yet, it is easy to help. I have taken a stand for Jesus by writing this book. You can make a difference by giving a copy to a family member, friends, neighbors, church members, or a person you may know who happen to be dealing with LGBT issues. Or will you, too, just look away?

Join in God's harvest for winning souls to Christ. In a plentiful harvest, the chances for success are great; we need not fail. So let's make a difference! For it is better to light one candle than to curse the darkness.

Also by Wayne McGhie, available on Amazon.com in paperback and Kindle format, and on all major online sites where books are sold.

Made in the USA
Columbia, SC
18 June 2020